WITHDRAWN

SKI

SOLDIER

A WORLD WAR II BIOGRAPHY

LOUISE BORDEN

CALKINS CREEK
AN IMPRINT OF HIGHLIGHTS
Honesdale, Pennsylvania

For information about permission to reproduce selections from this book,
please contact permissions@highlights.com.

Calkins Creek
An Imprint of Highlights
815 Church Street
Honesdale, Pennsylvania 18431
calkinscreekbooks.com
Printed in China

ISBN: 978-1-62979-674-1 (hc) • 978-1-68437-147-1 (eBook)
Library of Congress Control Number: 2018934182

First edition
10 9 8 7 6 5 4 3 2 1

Design by Red Herring Design
The text is set in Rockwell, Knockout, and Trade Gothic
The titles are set in Aku & Kamu.

For Cate, Marc, Abby, and Henry . . .
Morrie and Suzie . . .
the Seibert family . . .
and those of the 10th Mountain Division
who gave their lives in Italy.
We remember you.

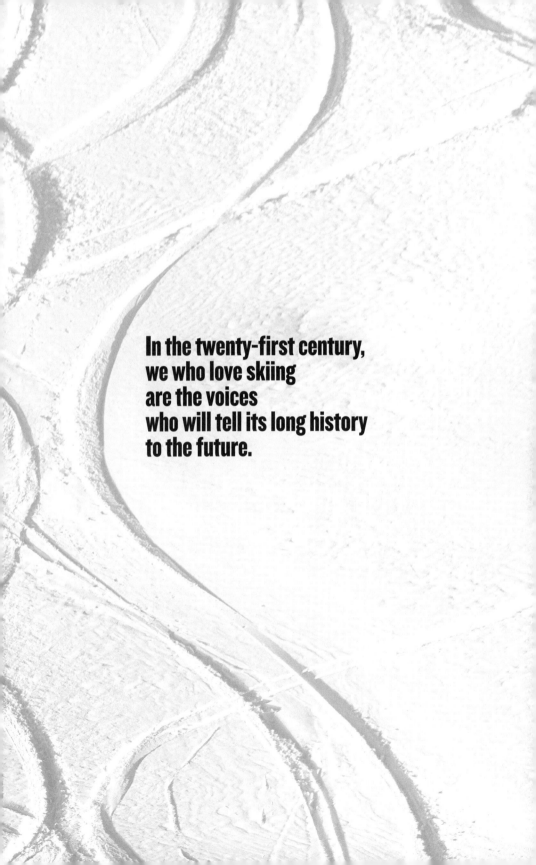

In the twenty-first century,
we who love skiing
are the voices
who will tell its long history
to the future.

KEY DATES
IN SKI SOLDIER: A WWII BIOGRAPHY

1939 to 1945—countries around the globe are caught up in a terrible conflict, World War II.

September 1, 1939—Adolf Hitler, leader of Nazi Germany, orders his troops to invade Poland.

September 3, 1939—Great Britain and France, allies of Poland, declare war against Germany.

1940—Italy and Japan join Germany and are known as the Axis Powers.

1940–1944—Germany occupies France.

December 7, 1941—Japan attacks the U.S. Naval Base in Pearl Harbor, Hawaii, and declares war on the United States.

December 8, 1941—the United States enters World War II.

December 11, 1941—Italy and Germany declare war on the United States. The United States joins Great Britain, the Soviet Union, and China (Allied Powers).

September 3, 1943—the Allies invade mainland Italy.

September 8, 1943—Italy surrenders to the Allies.

October 13, 1943—Italy declares war on Germany and joins the Allies.

June 5, 1944—the Allies liberate Rome, but Germany still occupies northern Italy.

December 1944—the first units of the 10th Mountain Division, part of the U.S. military effort, arrive in Italy.

February 1945—in the Apennines of northern Italy, soldiers of the 10th Mountain Division try the impossible on a string of peaks called Riva Ridge. *Ski Soldier* is the true story of one of those Americans.

AMERICA

One day in 1931,
seventeen miles southwest of Boston,
a boy named Peter Seibert
found a pair of skis and poles
in the loft of his family's barn.

They'd been made for his mother, Edythe,
when she was a child
and later stored away
with dusty harnesses.

There were no mountains near Sharon,
the town where the Seiberts lived.

But each winter
there was Massachusetts snow.

That morning
it glittered like sugar in Pete's front yard
and covered the rest of East Street.

Pete dragged the maple skis past the barn
and his family's small orchard
to the top of a rise
and slid his boots
into the leather toe straps.

Then . . . he pushed off.
Skiing!

To seven-year-old Pete Seibert,
there was nothing else like it in the world.

Christine and Pete Seibert, around three and four years old

Pete's sister, Christine, was a year younger.

Like Pete,
she'd been born in Sharon
where patriots cast cannon
to help win the American Revolution.

The Seibert kids knew well
the tale of their mother's ancestor,
Deborah Sampson,
whose portrait hung in their house.
Dressed in a man's shirt
and breeches she'd sewn herself,
Deborah joined the Continental Army
so she could fight the British redcoats.

Indeed,
the people of Sharon made history happen . . .

and Pete and Christine
would always be proud
that their words carried the tinge
of a New England accent.

Their father, Albert Seibert,
was an artist from Boston
and a man who loved adventure.

He'd driven west in a Model T Ford
and mined silver in Colorado,
high in the Rocky Mountains,
then returned home to marry Edythe.

In those hard times of the Great Depression,
Albert was lucky to have a job,
and on Sunday afternoons
he painted at his easel
while his wife tuned in to opera
on the radio.

Edythe Seibert had studied music
and now taught piano
in her living room
to many of the town's children.

But *Pete's* joy
was exploring the ponds and fields of Sharon,
and on snowy days
he crisscrossed the Seiberts' five acres
on his mother's old skis.

Albert Seibert

When he was nine,
Pete found seven-footers
under the family's Christmas tree.

New pine skis cost twenty dollars—
hours of piano lessons.

Pete gave the maple pair to Christine,
and that January
on the hills of Sharon
he showed his sister how to glide down
and snowplow to a stop.

The best places were Pettee's Hill
on Pleasant Street
and a slope edged by woods
near Upland Road,
both owned by Dr. Walter Griffin,
who took care of families
from birth to death.

The town's kids carried their sleds and skis
to the doctor's hills.
One of them, Morrie Shepard,
was in Pete's class
at Pleasant Street School.

Morrie was a skier,
and he soon became Pete Seibert's friend for life.

**Pete asked Dr. Griffin
if he could cut saplings
to make a trail in the woods
where the snow
was crisp and deep,
and the doctor let him.**

—MORRIE SHEPARD

Skis on their shoulders,
the two boys trudged past Norwood Street
and turned left on Upland
to the Griffin property.

They would pack the steep slope
by side-stepping,
then schuss straight down without turning . . .

or Pete would find sticks in the woods
and space them upright
in a zigzag line
down the snowy hill
to make a slalom course
the boys could weave through
on their skis.

Pete and Morrie would even ski after the sun went down.

Indeed,
they were ski crazy.

Centuries before Pete and Morrie
schussed Dr. Griffin's hill,
skis were used in Europe
to traverse snowy fields
and frozen lakes.
Soldiers even fought on skis
in winter battles.

When Pete Seibert was a boy,
alpine skiing—
skiing down a hill for fun—
was already a sport in Europe.
But in New England
the idea was still new.

With few rope tows or lifts,
American skiers had to climb their slopes
before they glided down.

For Pete,
anything about skiing was a magnet,
even the travel stories
he heard for the first time
on his mother's radio.

Lowell Thomas,
a famous broadcaster,
told of a resort in Sun Valley, Idaho,
and of downhill races in Austria's Alps.

Pete painted each picture in his mind.

White slopes dotted with skiers.

Lodges with wood eaves.

And alpine peaks
framed by blue sky.

Wonderful foreign words
like *christie* and *sitzmark*
drew Pete close to the world of mountains
and the sport he loved.

The Norwegian
christie: making a
turn and keeping the
skis parallel.

The German
sitzmark: a hollow
in the snow made
by a skier falling
backwards.

B_{y age thirteen}
Pete Seibert had made a promise:
someday
he would build his own resort . . .
with slopes and a lodge
and the *swish-swish* of skiers as they swept past.

On cold winter afternoons
Pete pictured his mountain
when he skied down a hill
to a neighbor's dairy barn
carrying two glass bottles . . .

and as he lugged them
back up the slope
with herringbone tracks,
filled with fresh milk
to deliver to his mother.

After school,
as he bagged groceries
to earn money,
Pete Seibert held tight
to his dream.

And always,
he waited for the season of snow.

In the late 1930s
Albert Seibert took a job
drawing forestry maps
in tiny Bartlett, New Hampshire,
almost two hundred miles
north of Sharon
and close to the state line of Maine.

This was ski country,
where snow covered the White Mountains
for months of the year.

A few miles from Bartlett,
in North Conway,
was a new ski area at Mount Cranmore.

And close by was Whitney's Hill,
with the first overhead cable tow
in the country.

Farther north
was Mount Washington,
the highest peak in New England.
Its steep bowl, Tuckerman Ravine,
drew the best racers,
who still had to climb three miles
to ski down.

Pete couldn't wait to carve his own path
on those New Hampshire slopes.

The first giant slalom race in
the United States was held at
Tuckerman Ravine in 1937.

The Seiberts kept their home in Sharon
and rented a farmhouse in Bartlett,
where Pete and Christine spent summers
and winter weekends.

On sunny days
when snow frosted the world white . . .

or on days
when the light was flat
and clouds changed the shadows
like quicksilver . . .

Pete was on his skis.

His new backyard had a hill
called Stanton Slopes
with something magical:
an eight-hundred-foot ski tow,
powered by a car engine.

Pete and Christine skied to the tow shed,
edged into a snowy track,
grabbed the moving rope,
and held on as it pulled them up the hill.

Now fifteen,
Pete was fearless on his skis.
He flew off homemade jumps
or schussed Stanton Slopes
until the sun slipped behind the White Mountains.

Pete never had to explain to his sister
his love of the sport.

All skiers share a bond:
the smell of snow on fir trees,
the perfect blue of mountain sky . . .

and the feeling of being *alive*.

Of being alone
even with a friend,
of forgetting everything else but skiing . . .

in sunlight or in shadow
as just one figure,
always looking ahead
to chart a path down.

In North Conway,
Pete Seibert signed up for local races.

Off the course,
he had a smile for all.

But on the course,
racers saw Pete's resolve.

He tied on a bib
with a number
over his wool sweater
and checked the bindings
that held his boots in place.

Then,
after tightening the strap
on his goggles,
Pete was ready.

Waiting his turn,
he didn't mind
the sharp wind or the cold.
Pete's focus was the line
he would ski down
with the fastest time.

Each second would be recorded by an official's watch.

3...2...1...Go!

Pete swept down the course,
guided by *real* slalom gates,
bamboo stakes that were taller than the sticks
on Dr. Griffin's hill back in Sharon.

Look ahead . . .

Pete planted his right pole,
then his left,
flying past each gate
before bending into a final tuck.

Amid the cheers of the spectators,
he blurred across the finish line
and slowed to a stop,
his gloved hands held high in victory.

**I was a tiger on the hill—
tough, grim,
and determined to win
every competition.**

—PETE SEIBERT

Toni Matt, 1939

But for Pete,
skiing wasn't just about racing.

It was part of something bigger:
the mountains.

Their silence and their sunshine.

Their storms and their seasons.

Their wide sky
and nights with a million stars.

This love of mountains
was Pete Seibert's true compass.

Over the next three winters,
the skiers who came to North Conway
became Pete's heroes.

Steve Knowlton and Percy Rideout
raced for their college teams.

Others were from Austria,
like the famous ski teacher
Hannes Schneider
and the racer Toni Matt.

They'd left their country
during dangerous times
as Adolf Hitler,
the *Führer*, or leader, of Nazi Germany,
plotted to take over Europe.

One April day at Tuckerman Ravine,
Toni Matt made history
by schussing the headwall at 80 miles per hour,
a feat never repeated . . .

and months later,
Hitler invaded Poland.

The date was September 1, 1939.

Far from Pete Seibert's mountains,
battles erupted across Europe.

France and Great Britain
were now at war with Germany.

At the local movie theater,
Pete and Christine
saw the startling newsreels
as Hitler's soldiers and their Panzer tanks
occupied Poland.

That November,
Finland was invaded by Russia
who had signed a pact with Germany.

Weeks later,
in his theater seat,
Pete watched the grainy films
of the outnumbered Finns
making daring attacks on skis or skates
to defend their lands . . .

and was riveted by the images
of white-clad soldiers
as they skied off into the forests.

By the spring of 1940,
Hitler's army seemed invincible
when Germany invaded Norway and Denmark . . .
and then, a month later,
Holland, Belgium, Luxembourg, and France.

German troops soon occupied them all.

That August
when Pete turned sixteen,
he saw newsreels of brave pilots
defending England's skies,
shooting down dozens of Hitler's planes.

The world watched
as the shadow of Nazi occupation
covered Europe . . .

as Italy and Japan became Hitler's allies . . .

as bombing and fires lit up London's nights . . .

and as the British people carried on with courage.

But when snow fell in New Hampshire
and the new year of 1941 began,
Hitler's war seemed far away
to Pete Seibert
when he laced up his boots
and flexed the tips of his skis.

There was only good powder
and this weekend's race
as he took a practice run
and came down the course,
turn after turn.

Skiing!

Pete Seibert (right) with ski friends Morrie Shepard (left) and Jimmy Ross (center) in New Hampshire, around 1941

December 7, 1941,
exactly four months
after Pete Seibert's seventeenth birthday,
Japanese planes
roared over the islands of Hawaii
in a surprise attack
on the American fleet at Pearl Harbor.

Pete was a senior
at Sharon High School,
and on that terrible Sunday,
Americans found Oahu
on their maps.
The island Japan had attacked
was almost three thousand miles west of California.

At noon the next day,
Pete, Christine, Morrie Shepard,
and all the other students at their school
filed into the hushed auditorium
to hear a live radio broadcast
as President Franklin Delano Roosevelt spoke to Congress.
Within an hour,
Congress declared war on the Empire of Japan.

War!

T hat week,
Germany and Italy joined Japan
against the United States.

Now, for America too,
it was a world war.

On the slopes in North Conway,
Pete Seibert heard talk of a man named Minnie Dole
who was helping the U.S. Army
scout for skiers, climbers, and outdoorsmen
to become soldiers.

Because Germany and Italy had mountain troops
and America had none,
Minnie had asked President Roosevelt
to create an army group
like Finland's
who'd fought their Russian
invaders . . .

ski troops who could defend
the north of America
or fight the enemy
in Europe's mountains.

Fourteen thousand men
were needed
to make one division.

Charles Minot "Minnie" Dole was a founder of
the National Ski Patrol, a volunteer group started
in 1938 to ensure safety on the slopes and
assist injured skiers.

New Hampshire's top skiers,
like Steve Knowlton and Percy Rideout,
soon enlisted in this special group.

So did Pete's hero Toni Matt,
the famous racer.

And Torger Tokle,
a Norwegian
and the champion ski jumper
of the world.

And Peppi Teichner,
a fine coach
who'd fled Nazi Germany.

Minnie Dole also recruited
hundreds of other Europeans
who'd come to America
to escape Hitler's rule.

**Pete is the ski champion of senior
and always seems happiest
when he is racing over a snowy slope or trail.
His ... sense of humor ...
submerged by his modest shyness,
comes flashing through from time to time
like sun shining through the clouds.**

—SHARON HIGH SCHOOL YEARBOOK

Now these ski stars
would train to be soldiers.

Too young to enlist,
Pete became an air raid courier at school
and helped with drills
showing students how to take cover.
He collected scrap metal
for the war effort,
still carrying in his heart
the vision
of his own ski resort.

But that was the far-off future.

Pete knew before he ever found his mountain,
he'd be in uniform . . .

serving his country.

In September of 1942,
the battle news was grim
in Europe and the Pacific
when Pete Seibert began an extra year of studies
at a boarding school in New Hampshire
a hundred miles north of Boston.
Then he would enlist.

At the New Hampton School,
Pete stowed his beloved skis
near the desk in his room
and pinned a photo of mountains
on the wall.

Through the winter of 1943,
he practiced on his skis,
carving his turns
or soaring into the air
from a snow-packed ramp.

Downhill,
jumping,
or cross-country,
Pete was a teammate
the New Hampton Huskies
could count on.

VARSITY SKI TEAM

The New Hampton Ski team had a very condensed wartime schedule. However, this did not interfere with the afternoon training. The spirit was one of the best and the number of members was large. The daily training followed a distinct schedule, so that every member would be in good condition in all four events. This year's team had the greatest number of boys go out for all four events. However, the traditional New Hampton weakness in cross country was present.

The two meets were with Kimball Union and Holderness. In the Kimball Union meet we were holding well until the cross country came. There the first one to place from our team came in thirteenth. In the jumping we could have done better, but due to the falling snow and very unusual jump we did not place as expected. Even though we came in the first places in slalom and downhill we lost the meet.

The meet with Holderness was at our home grounds so we were expected to do better. We placed first in all three events, cross country was not run, and in jumping out of the first six we took five. So we evened our score to one victory and one defeat.

MEETS

New Hampton	357.3	Kimball Union	377.5
New Hampton	298	Holderness	276

The varsity ski team trained each afternoon but, because of a limited wartime schedule, competed in only two meets. Pete is fifth from left.

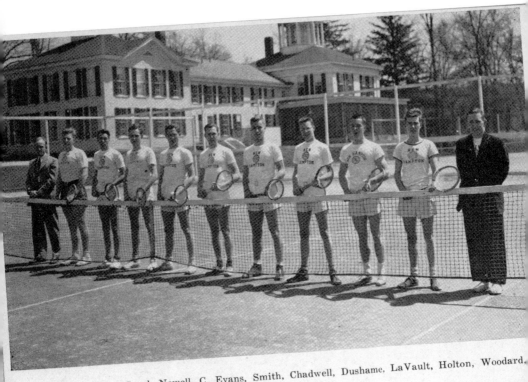

Left to right: Coach Newell, C. Evans, Smith, Chadwell, Dushame, LaVault, Holton, Woodard, Seibert, Lins, Manager Brenneke.

VARSITY TENNIS

The prospects of the tennis team look rather good, although we have been handi capped somewhat by a lack of warm weather. The team is off to a late start but we hop to play all our matches. Those which have been scheduled are with Holderness, Tilton and Kimball Union Academy. We will meet each team twice.

The following men are out for the team this year: Buckley Holton, Jesse Chadwel Bruce Lins, Stanton Smith, Frank Kimball, Peter Seibert, Norris Townsend, Robe Dushame and Melvin McLeod.

The competition will be extremely keen, but the spirit of the team is high and expect to live up to the exceptional record that our tennis teams have established in t past.

Mr. Newell will coach the team this year. He has had a great deal of tennis perience and we have promise of a very successful season.

The New Hampton School varsity tennis team welcomed Pete (third from right) because of his quickness on the court.

42

Pete played varsity football during his year at the New Hampton School (row two, second from right).

Back Row, left to right: Line Coach Shields, Managers Boyd and Friend, Backfield Coach Lombardy. Fourth Row: C. Evans, G. Faneuf, Black, Cooke, R. Faneuf. Third Row: Costello, Richart, Ball, Barrows, Prahm, Moore. Second Row: Gage, Kerr, Crone, Christgau, Siebert, Dushame. Front Row: Hill, Reusmann, J. Evans, Norris, Ward, Chase, Cates. Absent—Mixer and Mohrman.

VARSITY FOOTBALL

The Varsity football team had an even split for the season; it beat Andover, Clark and Tilton; it lost to K. U. A. twice and to Vermont once. The most thrilling contest was our 7-0 win over Tilton in the last few minutes of the game. Bill Black, one of the best players on the team, was lost for the season when he broke his collarbone. The majority of the team was made up of last year's men which included Captains Ward and Chase along with Evans, Norris, Cates, Reusmann, Hill, Cooke and Christgau. Some good new additions were Gage, Crone, Dushame and Faneuf.

The season was highly successful in that it was fun playing, and in keeping with wartime health needs the team members were placed in excellent physical condition. The .500 average the team established can't be compared with last year's record of six wins and one loss, but the defeat of Tilton was a standout in itself.

I

n May,
Pete packed up his books and his skis
and went home to his family.
He was eighteen
and old enough to serve.

On June 25,
Peter Werner Seibert signed papers
at the U.S. Army office in Boston
to join the group
of mountain troops
that Minnie Dole
had asked President Roosevelt
to create.
A few weeks later,
Pete reported to Ft. Devens,
an hour from Sharon.

The troopers had a name:
the 10th Light Division (Alpine).

The tiger on the hill
who'd won so many races
would now become
a soldier on skis.

Pete's senior picture in the 1943 New Hampton School yearbook, *The Belfry*

Peter Werner Seibert
"Pete"
Sharon, Mass.
Varsity Football (4); Ski
Team (4); Tennis (4); So-
cial Fraternity (4).
Service: Army

My reason for joining the 10th was to be in the mountains, summer or winter.... It was the country that I knew.

—PETE SEIBERT

Albert and Edythe Seibert
joined millions of other American families.

Their son had enlisted in the infantry.

Infantry meant the front lines of battle.
Infantry meant combat on foot.

In a khaki uniform and tie,
Pete left Ft. Devens
and boarded a troop train in Boston
that would chug across America
almost two thousand miles
to Denver, Colorado.

Then higher still
into the Rocky Mountains
to a new army base
eighteen miles from Leadville,
where Albert Seibert had mined silver
years before.

On July 12, 1943,
Pete Seibert reported
for duty at Ft. Devens.

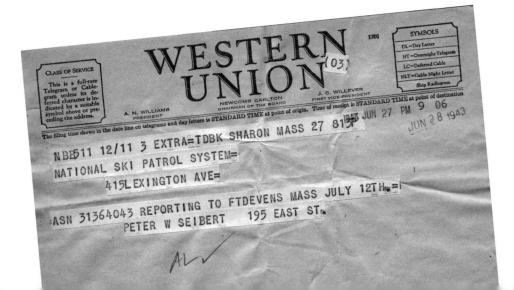

Camp Hale was in a valley
almost ten thousand feet above sea level
and framed by the tallest peaks
Pete Seibert had ever seen.

The three main dirt roads,
A, B, and C,
echoed with the rumble of trucks
and tramp of marching men.

There were rows of white buildings
called barracks
where each soldier was assigned a bunk.

There were stables for five thousand mules.

A kennel for two hundred sled dogs.

And Weasels,
odd black-and-white vehicles
that could be driven on snow.

Barracks at Camp Hale,
1943–1944

Pete's new army world
had rules and orders.

But he was among men
who shared his love of mountains
and who saw skiing as a way of life.
Pete's heroes were here
and wore the same uniform.

Steve Knowlton,
Percy Rideout,
and Torger Tokle
all served in the same
regiment as Pete—
the 86th—
along with almost
four thousand other men.

As a private in Company F
of the 86th,
Pete held the lowest rank.

But he had faith in himself
and in his skiing.

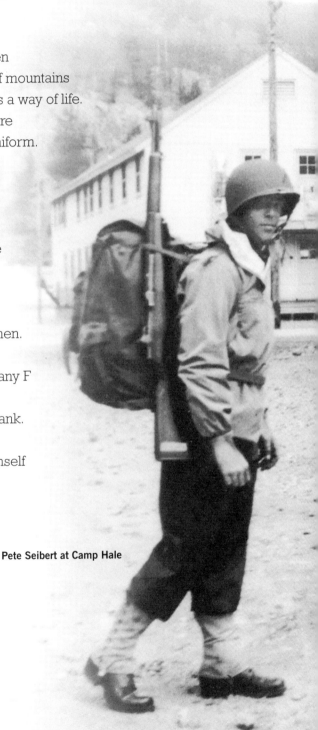

Pete Seibert at Camp Hale

That summer,
before the first snow at Camp Hale,
Pete Seibert learned the skills
of a good mountain soldier.

Company F was a rifle company,
so Pete spent hours of training
at the firing range,
loading and shooting his weapon,
a ten-pound M-1 rifle.

He learned how to dig a foxhole with a shovel
because it could save his life someday.

And he took classes in climbing.

Using hemp ropes
and steel spikes called pitons,
Pete learned how to ascend a rock face
and rappel down.

His instructors were experts
like Paul Petzoldt,
famous for his ascent of K2,
the second-highest mountain in the world.

Snowshoe training near Camp Hale

When autumn storms brought snow,
the two hundred men of Company F
pulled on fleece-lined hats
and reversible parkas:
white to hide them in the snow
and tan to blend in with the rocks.

Then they marched
higher into the mountains
to train at 12,500 feet.

Pete strapped on snowshoes
and slogged through drifts,
carrying a rucksack
with ninety pounds of gear.

He learned about avalanches
and how to build a snow cave,
and practiced moving wounded men
by toboggan or Weasel.

On bright days
Pete wore glacier glasses
to prevent snow blindness.
If he ever lost them,
he could now make eye shields
from the bark of trees.

Ski troopers with skis attached to their rucksacks, 1943–1944

And best of all,
Pete spent hours skiing.

Each soldier
had been given a pair of white poles
and white hickory skis
with bindings
to attach his boots to.

Six miles from Camp Hale
was Cooper Ski Hill,
a new training area
with the longest T-bar in the country,
built by army engineers.

It could pull skiers up
a mile and a half of slope.

Rank didn't matter on Cooper Hill.
Beginners had as their mentors
the very best.

With his smooth style and skill on skis,
Pete Seibert was chosen to teach
in the Mountain Training Group.

In the thin Colorado air
Pete, Steve Knowlton, and other instructors
showed novices in their regiment
how to put on skis,
how to step into the rutted track,
how to let the T-bar pull them to the top,
how to traverse the hill,
how to make a stem turn,
and how to snowplow to a stop.

Pete wanted his students
to find the same wonder of skiing
he'd felt as a boy
on Dr. Griffin's slope in Sharon.

Lesson in ski techniques at Camp Hale, 1943–1944

Coming down from Eagle Ridge near Camp Hale, during ski training, 1943–1944

Soldiers floundered in the snow
like turtles on their backs.
But with Pete as their model,
they learned to ski.

Each day while he trained for war
and taught others,
Pete looked at the peaks of the Rockies
as if for the first time.
He was a witness to their majesty,
and his love of mountains
was still his guide.

A hundred miles from Camp Hale,
along icy roads,
was the little town of Aspen
in the shadow of Ajax Mountain.

On weekends
Pete drove there with his friends
and paid fifty cents a day
to ride up the mountain
in a "boat lift"—
two toboggans lashed together,
with plank seats to sit on.

At the top
Pete gazed with awe
down the steep Roch Run.

Look ahead.

Then he swept through the powder
with balance and strength,
his legs and his skis
one with the mountain.

Skiing!

There was no sport like it in the world.

In the spring of 1944,
officers of Camp Hale's three regiments
planned mock battles
to test their new soldiers.

For almost a month,
from March into April,
thousands of men,
among them Pete Seibert,
skied or trekked
across miles of snow,
set up tents in blizzards,
and practiced battle plans.

Troopers, carrying full packs,
pause to rest during training.

To stay warm at 11,000 feet,
Pete tucked evergreen boughs
under his sleeping bag
and pulled his wet boots
inside the mummy sack
so they wouldn't freeze.

Mountain training trip from Leadville to Aspen, February 1944

Mountain soldiers in their camouflage whites

But Pete had stamina.
He'd survived the hardest training ever.

He was now a *true* mountain soldier.

As the Colorado snow melted
and Pete watched the slender aspens
unfold their green leaves
against the sky,
the tide of war turned.

In the Pacific,
America and her allies were sinking enemy ships
and in fierce battles,
freeing islands
that Japan had occupied.

In Europe,
the Allied side
was winning the air war
against Hitler.

More than a million soldiers trained in England.
Some of them ready to invade France.

Others advanced up the boot of Italy,
pushing back the German occupiers.

On June 5,
the radios at Camp Hale
crackled with President Roosevelt's voice:
Rome has been liberated!
Italy's capital was free.

But the Germans didn't surrender.
Everyone knew
they would move north
and set a line to block the Allies.

A day later,
Pete listened to the president again
as he led the nation in prayer.

With an armada of almost seven thousand ships,
Allied soldiers
had crossed the English Channel in the night.

Waves of thousands of planes flew above them.

The troops were now under fire,
wading onto the beaches of Normandy in France,
in a surprise invasion called D-Day.

There were more battles to come . . .
and Pete knew that someday soon
he'd carry his rifle,
and maybe his skis,
into combat.

But in late June
all the white skis and poles
were stored away.

Pete's 86th Regiment
and the rest of the troops
had orders to leave Camp Hale
and report to Camp Swift
near Austin.

There,
Pete and his ski pals
trained and trained
under the hot Texas sun.

Flat, dusty land.

Twenty-five-mile marches at night.

*Classes in artillery
and mortars,
bigger guns than rifles.*

Had the thousands of
mountain soldiers
been forgotten?

Camp Swift, Texas, where the 10th Mountain
troops were given "flatland" training in 1944.

60

With his calm voice,
quick reflexes,
and focus on each drill,
Pete Seibert was seen as a leader of men
in Company F
during his training at Camp Swift.

That August,
by Special Order 191,
Pete was promoted to platoon sergeant,
skipping over the rank of corporal.

He was now in charge of forty men.

Train.
Train.
March.
March.

Each night,
as the Texas sun
sank slowly below the horizon,
Pete missed the Rockies
and always
the adventure of skiing.

Like a stirring autumn wind,
the ski troops were renamed
on November 6:
the 10th Mountain Division.

Pete Seibert now had a new patch,
the word MOUNTAIN,
to sew on his uniform sleeve.

This shoulder insignia, or badge, was issued to all 10th Mountain soldiers to wear on their sleeves for overseas duty in the 1940s.

And on Thanksgiving Day,
the 10th had a new top commander,
George P. Hays.

The gutsy general had orders for his troops:
overseas, to combat.
But *where* was kept secret.

At the end of November,
Pete's 86th Regiment
was the first
to leave Camp Swift by train.

George P. Hays earned a Medal of Honor for bravery in World War I. In World War II, he fought at Omaha Beach during the D-Day invasion.

Three days later,
the 86th arrived near Yorktown,
where George Washington's army
had defeated the British.
The regiment awaited new orders
at Camp Patrick Henry,
an army base named for the famous patriot.

Here on the Chesapeake Bay,
lines of waterfowl crossed the sky.
The Virginia air was soft
and the land was laced
by creeks and tides.

On December 11,
hours before dawn
from a dock in Newport News,
five thousand soldiers
boarded the SS *Argentina*.

Pete wore his helmet
and carried a pocketknife
in his trousers
and a pistol
on his leather belt.

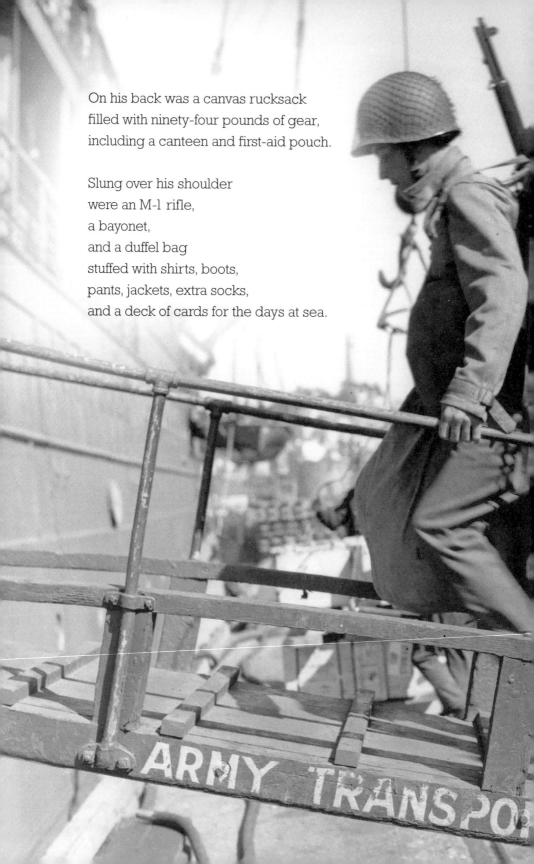

On his back was a canvas rucksack
filled with ninety-four pounds of gear,
including a canteen and first-aid pouch.

Slung over his shoulder
were an M-1 rifle,
a bayonet,
and a duffel bag
stuffed with shirts, boots,
pants, jackets, extra socks,
and a deck of cards for the days at sea.

What impressed me was walking up that gangplank. They read out your last name and you give your first name and you step up on that gangplank, you know things are getting serious.

—FRAN LIMMER, COMPANY A, 86TH INFANTRY REGIMENT

A soldier boards a transport ship for overseas duty in the 1940s.

OCEAN

T

he destination of the *Argentina*
was still a secret
when the ship set sail at 8 a.m.,
cruising through the waters
of the blue-gray Hampton Roads
and into the Atlantic,
protected by a convoy of U.S. Navy ships.

Wearing a life jacket,
Pete stood on deck
as the shores of America faded from sight.

Where was his troopship headed?

It had to be Europe.

Or maybe Burma to fight the Japanese.
Burma had mountains.

The 10th Mountain Division was fit
but *green*—
the men had never seen a German
or Japanese soldier.

What would combat be like . . .
to shoot at the enemy
or have a gun rattle
a thousand real bullets
at your platoon?

That night,
Pete Seibert and his men
slept below on metal bunks
stacked three to ten high
as the *Argentina* surged on
into ocean darkness.

Before their life in the army,
most of them
hadn't been beyond their home states.
Now they were crossing an ocean.

With his New England accent
and his humor,
Pete gave unspoken courage to his men.

Halfway across the Atlantic,
a rumor was made official:
the ship was going to *Italy*.

During the slow days at sea,
Pete tried to imagine
what lay ahead.

H

He knew the advance against the Germans
north of Rome
had been road by road
and house by house.

That the boom of guns
echoed across the Apennine Mountains
as the Americans and British
tried to break the line
that Hitler's troops held.

When night shaded the horizon,
Pete watched schools of fish
cast a glow
by each side of the *Argentina* . . .
a marvel of the ocean
as grand as mountain light.

One morning,
Pete and other soldiers crowded on deck
to stand by the ship's railing.

Land!

On the left, to port,
were the hills of Spain,
dotted with clusters of white houses.

On the right, to starboard,
was Tangier,
a town in Morocco,
with a smudge of beach
and more white houses.

Pete's convoy
was passing between two continents,
Europe and Africa.
Here,
less than ten miles of water parted them.

The *Argentina* plowed on
through the Strait of Gibraltar,
past the famous rock and naval base
that guarded the entrance
to the Mediterranean Sea,
a brighter blue
than the navy swells of the Atlantic.

More than two hundred years earlier,
the British had won the territory of Gibraltar
in a treaty with Spain.
Royal Air Force Beaufighters
swept over the convoy with a roar
and waggled their silver wings in welcome.

Pete Seibert stayed on deck
to watch the gleaming planes
circle back to their base.

He always looked ahead:
as a racer
to the finish line . . .
and as a soldier
to each mission.

And like those pilots,
he would do his duty.

The *Argentina* finally anchored at night
in the harbor of Naples,
south of Rome.

It was December 22,
and tomorrow
back in New England,
Christine Seibert would turn nineteen.

A few lights winked along the Italian shore,
and after checking his gear,
Pete lay awake in his ship bunk.

Would he survive?
Would he ever see his kid sister again?

**We were in a rifle company
and we knew darn well
we'd be right in the thick of it.
It was gonna happen.**

—PETE SEIBERT

ITALY

The next morning
was the day before Christmas Eve.

Leaving the *Argentina*,
the 86th Regiment
filed down a ramp
to a battered wharf.

The forty men of Pete Seibert's platoon,
close as brothers
after months of training,
were looking to him for orders.

Duffel bag and M-1 in hand,
Pete scanned the harbor.
The bombs of Allied planes
had done their work
on every Naples dock and pier,
and the Germans, in retreat,
had blown up ships and sheds.

Children in ragged clothes
scavenged for scraps of food
along the docks.
In the cold day,
some were barefoot.

This was the toll of war.

That night,
Percy Rideout,
now a captain in Company F,
passed on orders to Pete
and his other platoon leaders
to set up camp near Naples.

Pete moved among his men
as they unpacked their gear
in a half-built orphanage . . .
men like Private Howie Schless,
who was a buddy of Pete's.

Howie didn't carry a rifle.
He was a medic,
and his job would be to tend the wounded.

Later,
wrapped in two blankets,
a weary Sergeant Seibert
spent his first night in Italy
on a cold marble floor.

The day after Christmas,
the troops crammed onto a rusty freighter,
the *Sestriere*.

It had a wood mast and shabby lateen sail,
a pale red triangle
that was unfurled
to catch the wind and add speed.

Billowing smoke from its old engine,
the *Sestriere* sailed north
up the Italian coast
for a day and a night
until it arrived in Livorno,
the harbor the Americans called Leghorn.

As in Naples,
Livorno's docks and squares
had been smashed by bombs of the Allies
during the battles to free the town
from the Germans.

After a few days near Pisa
with its famous leaning tower,
Pete and his men rode north in army trucks
past medieval Lucca
to the front line of the Allied armies.

Along the way,
the roads were scarred by rubble.
Each village was so different
from Sharon or Bartlett.

Pete Seibert waved to the skinny kids
who called *Americano! Americano!*
when his truck rumbled by.

Many of the Italians he passed
had first stood with Nazi Germany.

Now Italy
had surrendered to the Allies
and had switched sides
to fight against the Germans.

But the battles were far from over.

Even though the Allies had liberated
Rome and Naples,
Livorno and Lucca,
Hitler's soldiers still held much of Italy.

To the north of Lucca,
they occupied the Apennine Mountains.

German troops
were dug in along the peaks
in a strong line across Italy
from east to west.
From their high posts
they could check any advance
by the Allied armies.

If soldiers or trucks or jeeps
moved in daylight,
German artillery guns
fired on them.

And the enemy kept watch over Highway 64,
the road to the town of Bologna
that led on to the Po Valley,
rich with farms that supplied
Hitler's soldiers with food.

**10th Mountain troops debark at
Leghorn, Italy, in 1945. From there,
they head north to the Apennines.**

T
hat January,
as the rest of the 10th Mountain Division
crossed the Atlantic
to join the 86th Regiment,
General Hays set up his headquarters
in the hilltop village of San Marcello.

He and his mountain troops
had been sent to Italy to do a job:
break through the German line.

Three times already,
Allied forces
had tried to capture Mount Belvedere,
a few miles away . . .
a big mountain held by the enemy.

Three times they'd failed.

Belvedere was the key
to opening the door to other mountains,
and then the Po Valley.

Now it was winter—
impossible to push forward.

This pen and ink sketch—*Convoy*—was
drawn in Italy by artist Wilson Ware who
served as an officer in the 86th Regiment.
Note the sign to San Marcello.

CONVOY

WWARE/45

A patrol of the 86th Regiment pauses
to strap on snowshoes.

But with his well-trained men,
General Hays didn't need to wait
for spring weather.

He gave orders
to do reconnaissance:
scout the German line
and search for the German posts.

Only a few miles north
of the general's San Marcello command post
were three small villages:
Cutigliano,
Ontoni,
and Vizzaneta.

Pete Seibert and the men in Company F
soon knew these hill towns by heart.

They moved into farmhouses
and foxholes
where, earlier,
shivering British soldiers had lived
as *they* patrolled the German line.

Now Pete had his first good look
at Italy's mountains.

The Apennines weren't as high as the Rockies,
but they were beautiful . . .
with more trees,
and red-roofed towns
tucked into the snowy landscape.

The front line
was in the middle of the mountains.
Snowdrifts up to twenty feet deep filled the ravines.

A no-man's-land
ran between the American posts
and the Germans at the top of the peaks.

Hidden in a stone house during the day,
Pete Seibert used his field glasses
to locate German sentries
high on the peaks
where they scanned the villages below
with their telescopes.

He studied maps
and talked with *partigiani*.
These brave partisans lived in the hills
and fought with the Allies,
serving as guides
on paths they knew well.

At night,
Pete's platoon was busy.
Patrols of eight or ten men,
usually with a partisan,
went out into the windy darkness
along the base of the German-held peaks.

Pete led his men across the ravines
on snowshoes,
since the land was too steep for skis.

No flashlights were allowed.
No match could be struck.

Then he sent his scouting reports
back to headquarters in San Marcello.

One of the few patrols of the 86th Regiment to use skis. Snowshoes were better in the steep terrain.

Wearing boots caked with snow
or mud,
Pete and his platoon
shared cold rations of food
and dozed under their wet blankets.

These mountains *were* beautiful . . .
but the enemy owned the peaks,
and night or day
they held danger.

In San Marcello,
General Hays studied photos of Mount Belvedere
taken by American pilots.

He saw that *near* Belvedere
was a three-and-a-half-mile spine
of other peaks
also held by the Germans . . .
a spine the Allies had never tried to capture.

With the wide view from this spine
the enemy could warn soldiers
on Mount Belvedere
whenever the Allies advanced.

This was why the three attacks had failed.

And the sheer sides of this spine of peaks
kept the Germans safe
on high ground.

Only expert climbers
could scale those walls of rock.

DAWN, PATROL, ROCCA CORNETA

Wilson Ware's *Dawn, Patrol, Rocca Corneta*, 1945. This small hill town was near Vidiciatico, in the area of Mt. Belvedere.

Each peak in the spine
had a difficult Italian name
like Pizzo di Campiano.

But Riva,
a small mountain just to the north,
was so easy to say
it became the Americans' nickname
for *all* the peaks
along the three-and-a-half-mile line:

Riva Ridge.

General Hays knew
he must capture Riva Ridge
and take those observation posts.

If his men made the ascent
in the dark of night,
and if they all reached the top of the ridge
at the same time
without the Germans knowing,
the Americans could mount a surprise attack
the next morning.

Some of the climbs
would be as high as 2,200 feet.

If the attack failed, many could die.

A 10th Mountain jeep with Riva Ridge in the background

General Hays and his staff sketched a secret plan.

Five groups of soldiers from the 86th,
including Pete Seibert's Company F,
would attack Riva Ridge.

The rest of the regiment
would stay hidden
in the town of Vidiciatico.

In the days before the assault,
each group would have its patrols
scout one path up the rocky ridge.

Each of these five paths
had to be wide enough
for two hundred men to climb
in single file.

If the attack worked
and Riva Ridge was captured,
General Hays would send
the 85th and 87th regiments
to capture Mount Belvedere.

At night
Pete Seibert pulled on
his white anorak
and his fleece cap . . .
and joined others
to search Riva Ridge
and locate trails for the attack.

**For more than a week
we scouted Riva Ridge,
rock by rock.**

—PETE SEIBERT

RIVA RIDGE
February 18 - 25

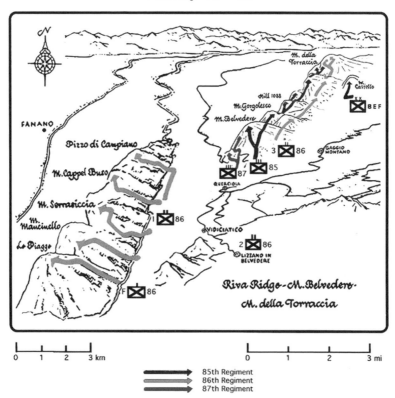

0 1 2 3 km

0 1 2 3 mi

85th Regiment
86th Regiment
87th Regiment

Map with five trails up Riva Ridge

At first
the patrols couldn't find *any* paths up.

Just ice, fog, and deep snow.

Finally
the scouts located two trails
that would lead to the top.

Then,
three more.

The final plan was kept secret
until one week before the attack.

Each peak on Riva Ridge
was given a ski word as a code name.

Pizzo di Campiano was SNOWPLOW,
to be taken by a platoon of Company A
on Trail #1.

Mount Cappel Buso was STEM TURN,
to be taken by Company B
on Trail #2.

Ridge X and *Serrasiccia* were CHRISTIE,
to be taken by Company C
and two units of Company D
on Trail #3.

Mancinello and *Le Piagge* were SITZMARK,
to be taken by the rest of Company A
on Trail #4
and Company F on Trail #5.

Lieutenant Colonel Henry J. Hampton, who served as
the commander of the 1st Battalion, 86th Mountain
Infantry Regiment, signed the Riva Ridge attack order.

Pete and Company F
left their posts on the front line
and were sent to the town of Lucca
to practice climbing in a rock quarry.

Pete's commander, Percy Rideout,
handed out more maps to his soldiers.
Together,
they studied a table model of Riva Ridge
that had been made to scale
by an officer in the 86th.

In planning the mission,
every detail was important.

What the men would carry.
Whether fixed ropes were needed on the trails.
How to contact each company
if it reached the top.
How to carry wounded men
down the rocks of the ridge.
How to get supplies up the trails
if the ridge was taken.
How to move twelve thousand men into position
for two surprise attacks
without the enemy knowing.

After a week in Lucca
it was time to head back to the line.

Trucks, jeeps, guns, mules, shovels, soldiers . . .
all were soon on the move at night,
along twisting miles of rutted roads
that cut through the stony land.

As his platoon marched along,
Pete Seibert felt the silence
and grandeur of the dark Apennines.

Long ago other soldiers
had trod the same roads
and crossed the same stone bridges.

These mountains held their stories
and would soon hold his.

Company F moved into Vidiciatico,
a village with a thousand-year-old tower
in the main square.

To the right
was a view of the prize,
Mount Belvedere.

To the left, to the northwest,
was the rugged outline of Riva Ridge.

Vidiciatico, Italy, in 1945
with Mt. Belvedere in the
background. The thousand-
year-old tower was damaged
by shellfire during the war.

Wilson Ware's *1st Battalion Command Post, Vidiciatico*, 1945. Soldiers of the 10th Mountain Division gathered in this town to plan the attacks on Riva Ridge and Mt. Belvedere.

The Italians in Vidiciatico wanted peace.
They welcomed the American troopers
into their houses.
It was a time of hiding
for Pete and his platoon.

Shutters were closed during the day.

Shy children stood in the doorways
and were given milk and food
by the Americans.
Some ran messages for the soldiers
along the icy streets.

Raymond Roux
of the 87th
Regiment offers
food to children in
Vidiciatico, Italy,
February 1945.

The rest of the 10th Mountain Division
camped in other villages
to ready for the attack.

On February 15,
an American scout plane
flew over Riva Ridge
to study the peaks a final time.

The winter storms had swept past,
and the deep drifts had melted
into patches of stony mud,
but there was still snow on top.

During each night of waiting,
Pete Seibert saw a false moonglow
shine across Mount Belvedere and Riva Ridge.

From seven miles behind Vidicatico,
American soldiers beamed searchlights
toward the walls of Riva Ridge
to blind the Germans on top.
Pete was glad for the spooky glow—
it was safer for moving about and gathering supplies.

Early on February 17,
before the sun was up,
Pete led his platoon across muddy fields
and settled into hiding places
in the tiny hamlet of Madonna Dell'Acero.

He looked ahead . . . to the mission.

Le Piagge was the 5,000-foot peak
Company F had orders to capture.

Below it,
the waters of the Dardagna River
churned white through a gorge.

That night,
Captain Rideout sent a patrol
to make a crossing of logs and rocks.
Pete and his men slept outdoors,
wrapped in blankets,
or in the cold attics of Madonna Dell'Acero.

February 18, 1945.
Pete moved among his men,
sharing courage.

That afternoon,
Trail #4 was scrapped.
It was too steep for two hundred men to climb.
Company A would now use #5,
then veer to Mount Mancinello.
They would leave three hours before
Company F.

Pete checked his watch
as the minutes ticked past.
Then it was "H Hour"—
code for when the bold plan would begin.

At 7:30 p.m.,
Company A moved out.

Soon Pete and Company F
and the rest of the attack force
would head toward their assigned trails.

For the enemy atop Riva Ridge,
it was an ordinary night.
The Americans had their searchlights on.
The Germans sensed motion along the roads below,
but every night
their enemy rustled about.

Pete Seibert checked his watch again.
It was 10 p.m.

His platoon and Company F were ready.

Move out . . .
The words were whispers
from officers to privates.
Then, no one spoke.
Some soldiers chewed gum
to prevent any coughs.

On each man's helmet
was a piece of silver tape.
The luminous strip would guide the men
and help them know friend from foe.

Pete Seibert carried his own fear inside.

So did Percy Rideout and Howie Schless
and every one of Pete's friends in Company F.

P̲ete had the same focus
as he did in a ski race.

Look ahead.

In his mind,
he went over each step of the mission.

Cross the Dardagna.
Find the trail,
scale the rocks,
help others do the same.
Make no noise,
listen for enemy dogs,
gain the top of the peak.
Contact Company A, to the right.
Remain silent until 7:30 a.m.

Then . . .
Attack the posts.
Take prisoner those who surrender.
Hold the peak of Le Piagge,
the left flank of Riva Ridge,
until replaced by units in Company A.

Pete carried his M-1
with a steel bayonet for silent combat,
his heavy rucksack,
and extra rounds of ammunition.

And so did each man on the trail—
except the medics like Howie Schless,
who had red crosses on their helmets
and carried no weapons,
only bandages
and bags of life-saving plasma.

In the gloom,
Pete stepped into the swirling current
of the Dardagna
and clambered over slick rocks and logs.

At that moment,
hundreds of other men
were wading into the river
and trekking toward their attack trails.

The searchlights had been switched off,
and above Pete
the mountains were as black as ink
in the night mists.

Suddenly,
a soldier in Pete's platoon slipped,
flailing under his pack
in the icy Dardagna.
In a quick moment,
Pete jumped in
and hauled the injured man to a nearby shed.

There, Pete pulled on dry socks
and hurried back to lead his platoon.

For the next five hours,
almost a thousand American soldiers
inched their way
up the cold sides of Riva Ridge.

On two of the four paths,
fixed ropes were tapped into the rocks
by advance climbers,
their hammers muffled with cloth.

The only sound Pete heard
was the hard breathing
and grunts of his men.
Doubled over with their packs,
they pulled themselves up
rock after rock.

When a soldier's boot
sent pebbles rattling in the night,
Pete flinched and held his breath
as each echo faded away.

Heart thumping,
he slithered over the top of Le Piagge
with his men close behind him.

It was 3:55 a.m.

It was *all* scary.

—PETE SEIBERT

In a whisper,
Captain Rideout made contact
with Company A,
now atop the next peak, Mancinello.

Pete spotted an enemy snow cave
yards away . . .
a good place for Germans to camouflage their guns.
He listened for the bark of a guard dog
or a German voice,
but all was quiet.

Pete's platoon silently dug shallow holes
into the snowy ledges.
Then,
curled against the cold,
the men waited for dawn.

Pete went over the details of the attack.
Forty men were counting on him.

The minutes passed,
and in the early morning
thick fog drifted across the crest of Le Piagge . . .
a perfect screen to hide Company F.

At 7:30 a.m.,
the attack began on each peak.

With catlike steps,
Pete Seibert and his men crossed the frozen ground,
bayonets and grenades at the ready.

As the rising sun burned off the mist,
Company F rushed the scattered huts,
waking German soldiers.
Pete unclipped the grenade in his hand
and hurled it toward a cabin.

Hitler's soldiers scrambled to man their guns
and resist the attack.
The rattle of machine guns
and steady bullets from M-1 rifles
tore through the morning fog.

Pete and the others in Company F
flattened into firing positions,
their white jackets
hiding them against the snow.

Across the six peaks,
the enemy was outnumbered.
Some lost their lives.
Others were taken prisoner.

All were stunned
that so many Americans
had climbed the impossible east side
of Riva Ridge.

General Hays had feared
that hundreds would be killed or wounded.
Not one of his soldiers died
in the climb to the top.

On Pizzo di Campiano,
the Germans fought back for four days
but then surrendered.

With the capture of Riva Ridge,
the Americans had broken one strong link
of the Nazi chain that held Italy.

Pete Seibert,
his platoon,
his company,
his captain,
and hundreds in the 86th Regiment
were part of it.

At 11:30 p.m. the next night,
the surprise attack on Mount Belvedere began.

This time,
other ski troopers did the climbing.

When they reached the peak,
there were fierce firefights.
Belvedere had more Germans on top
and many guns.

That afternoon,
hundreds of Italians lined their fields
to watch the battle rage on the mountain.

Troopers who had climbed Riva Ridge
stayed to protect the peaks,
and American engineers
built an aerial tram
in record time
to carry up supplies.

Company F was relieved on Le Piagge
by units on Mount Mancinello,
and Pete Seibert and his men
threaded their way
down the steep rocks
and back across the Dardagna.

The platoon hadn't slept in two days,
and they were hungry.
This time,
they passed by their hiding places
in Madonna Dell' Acero
and returned to Vidiciatico.

Company F soon had a front-row seat:
American planes crossed the sky,
helping the 85th and 87th capture Mount Belvedere.

To celebrate the climb of Riva Ridge,
Pete Seibert,
still in his combat boots,
borrowed skis from the supply post
in Vidiciatico
and found a slope of soft snow.

There, with his army pals,
he marked a slalom course with sticks.

Even in a war zone
with the combat on Belvedere
just two miles away,
Pete still loved mountains.

With the tower of Vidiciatico
tall against a pewter sky,
Pete flew through the course of sticks.

Litter bearers evacuate the
wounded on Mt. Belvedere.

Returning from
the front lines on
Belvedere

Capturing Riva Ridge and Mount Belvedere
had opened the door
to the rest of the German line.

Company F had new orders:
march northeast and prepare for combat.

Captain Rideout showed Pete
and another sergeant, Ed Hutchins,
a map of the string of peaks
General Hays wanted to capture.

This time,
the 10th Mountain Division
would attack together.

Company F's mission
was to advance on Mount Terminale.

A squall of sleet and snow
swirled across the roads,
and Pete's platoon was sodden and tense.

Pete cleaned his rifle
and hunkered down,
waiting for the weather to clear.

After the sleet stopped,
the attack began
early on the morning of March 3.

Guns boomed
and Company F moved out
over the muddy ground,
slick with ice,
toward Mount Terminale.

Pete watched as a grove of trees
was torn from the mountainside
by artillery fire.

He knew that not far away
Italian families
were cowering in bomb shelters
in the town of Iola,
while German and American guns
traded death.

These mountains that stirred him
with their splendor
were now marked by war
and stained with blood.

Soon the mortar fire from the Germans
was so intense
that Pete ordered his platoon
to take cover near a stone farmhouse.

The ground shook from more rounds
of the enemy guns
and the awful roar.

Pete Seibert checked on his men,
his platoon of brothers,
and called their names
with instructions.

Suddenly,
a mortar blast shattered a nearby tree
and Pete was thrown to the ground,
hit by shards of wood and metal shrapnel
that tore through his helmet,
split open his nose,
and knocked out some of his teeth.

His left arm was almost cut in half
at the elbow,
and his right leg was sliced open.

In a cloud of pain and blood,
Pete tried to stand but fell back.

Shocked faces passed above him,
and he heard voices.

Ed Hutchins was there.

You'll be okay, Pete.
Lie back, you're okay.

But his eyes held other words.

Then Howie Schless was next to him
with his kit and bandages
and a shot of morphine
to dull the terrible pain.

Howie worked with sure hands
and never left Pete's side.

Thirty minutes later,
a second blast
thundered over the farmhouse
and spun Howie away,
tearing open his shoulder.

Pete was also hit . . .
this time in his chest
and again in his right leg.

Still trying to help his wounded sergeant,
the medic from Philadelphia collapsed.

In the haze of the morphine,
Pete saw two Company F medics
carry Howie away.

Alone,
he crawled through the icy mud
toward some logs
until another medic
zigzagged across the shaking earth
to lie next to Pete as a shield.

The enemy shelling went on and on,
ripping up the rocky land
as two medics put Pete on a stretcher
to take him to a farmhouse,
the aid station for the 86th.

Finally,
they carried Pete past two jeeps
parked in a courtyard
and through a doorway.

Inside the house,
Pete was gently lifted onto a table,
and the men used their skill
to dress his wounds.

As more shells shook the walls,
the medics pulled Pete under the table
and huddled beside him.

Later,
wrapped in bandages,
Pete was loaded on a litter
and into a jeep.
The medics held him down
as they bounced along the stony trails . . .

away from the battle,
away from the guns,
away from the trembling mountainsides . . .

away from the war.

Pete was taken to an aid station
safe behind the battle line
where doctors worked to save his left arm
and salvage what was left
of his kneecap.
American army nurses fed him
through a tube.

Both of his eyes were bandaged,
and he was given shots
eight times a day.
Time blurred by in a fog of penicillin
until Pete woke up in a hospital
in Livorno.

Now,
only one of his eyes was covered.

Hundreds of 10th Mountain troopers
were killed in action
as the division broke through
the last of the Apennine peaks,
crossed the Po River,
and pushed north to Lake Garda
in the Alps.
And like Peter Werner Seibert,
thousands were wounded.

Weeks after he was injured,
the ski racer who'd led his platoon
up the rock sides of Le Piagge
was finally able to feed himself
with one hand.

In April 1945, the 10th Mountain troops were near Lake Garda, the largest lake in Italy.

For almost two months,
Pete would stay in the hospital in Livorno.

Fighting the pain, he could sit up:
a small step in his mission
to recover.

But his legs.
His knee.

In Pete's restless sleep
and jumbled dreams,
there were mountains
and slopes
and Colorado snow.

Skiing was his *life* . . .
and the army doctors warned him
he'd be lucky just to walk.

Each day,
surrounded by men
who'd lost an eye or a limb
or—worse—their spirit,
Pete refused to picture a future
without skis.

Looking ahead
was something he was good at.

The hospital radio was full of war news . . .
and sadness.

On April 12,
President Franklin Delano Roosevelt,
the man who'd led America
since Pete was eight years old,
died in Georgia.

Pete Seibert and the men in his ward wept.
On that day especially,
they felt far from home.

On April 30,
Adolf Hitler took his own life
in a bunker in Berlin
and a few days later,
his army in Italy surrendered
to Allied forces.

The end of the Nazi grip was near,
and Germany soon signed a full surrender.

The long war in Europe was over,
but Pete's mission to heal his wounds was not.

OCEAN

The same week
that the cities of Europe
rang bells of freedom,
Pete Seibert was carried aboard a hospital ship.

For the two-week voyage home,
he couldn't leave his metal bunk
or go on deck to see the sky.

What would his mother say
about the raw scars on his face?

About the stitches and gauze?

And his legs,
once so strong and so fast?

Pete listened as the men near him
moaned with pain
and the smell of wounds
filled the close air.

The unknown was before him,
as wide as an ocean
with an empty horizon.

Could he ski again?

Arriving in port
near Hampton Roads,
Pete lay on a stretcher
on the Virginia dock
among rows of other helpless men.

Each soldier wore a tag
with his name and his destination.

Pete Seibert's was a hospital
that mended bones and muscles
in Martinsburg, West Virginia.

Unable to move or walk,
Pete gazed up at the blue sky
and heard the sounds of the harbor,
alive with boats and peace.

He was home in America.

He'd climbed Riva Ridge
in a far corner of the world
and survived the war.

Nothing was impossible.

**What makes life
interesting
are challenges.
And as you might guess,
I love a challenge.**

—PETE SEIBERT

AMERICA

August 7, 1945,
the day that Pete turned twenty-one in West Virginia,
was bittersweet.

The hospital radio was somber
with historic news:
a day earlier,
America had dropped an atomic bomb
on Japan.

A week passed,
and on August 15
Emperor Hirohito's voice
was heard for the first time by his people
as he announced Japan's surrender
in a broadcast.

In Martinsburg,
Pete's summer victory had been learning to stand.

Over the months,
army surgeons had worked
on Pete's legs and knee.

If he could stand . . .
he could walk.

And if he could walk . . .
he could ski.

Behind his quips to the nurses
and his crooked smile,
Pete carried his pain.

But after each operation,
he was closer to his goal,
and his deep will
was a stubborn gleam of sun
on the long days.

One step.

Practice.

Now one more.

And one more.

With every new step,
Pete was crossing that ocean
to the future.

The goal of his mission . . .

to ski again.

In October,
as the leaves turned red and yellow
in New England,
Pete was allowed to go home
for a short visit.
His parents had left Bartlett at war's end
and were back in Sharon.

In his khaki tie and overcoat,
Pete leaned on a cane
and limped past the lamppost
in his yard.

Albert, Edythe, and Christine
were all there waiting for him.

To Nick and Chris Dann,
the two boys who lived across the street
and loved to sled on Dr. Griffin's hills,
their neighbor was a hero.

After ten more months
of surgeries,
this time in Valley Forge, Pennsylvania,
Pete came back to Sharon for good.

Seventeen months had passed
since that morning in Italy.

Morrie Shepard was home from the war, too.
He saw past the red scars
that were healing on Pete's face.

Instead,
the two skiers talked about the future.

Aspen.

That was the place.

In the fall of 1946,
Pete stepped from a train platform
in Denver
and looked west.

The Colorado Rockies lined the horizon,
and there was already snow on the far peaks.

Even without his kneecap,
skiing was going to be part
of Pete's life.

And he hadn't let go of his promise.

Someday.

THE PROMISE

On cold winter mornings,
the operators
who ran the new chairlift on Ajax Mountain,
the longest in the world,
would stand and watch Pete . . .

moving through powder
as if he owned it,
carving his turns down the slope.

The lone figure
skied in his own unique way,
with his legs
almost locked together.

Everyone in Aspen knew Pete Seibert,
who now taught in the new ski school
begun by Friedl Pfeifer.
Veterans of the 10th Mountain
filled the small town,
and some taught skiing with Pete.

Friedl Pfeifer skied to and from school as a boy in Austria. He left his country in 1938 for America, served in Italy in the 87th Regiment of the 10th Mountain Division, and headed the ski school in Aspen from 1946 until the mid-1960s.

For weeks,
they'd seen him practice on the mountain.

And then,
as Pete slowly returned to racing,
they'd seen him win.

First a downhill . . . then a slalom.

Percy Rideout skiing
in Aspen, 1947

Pete jumping in Aspen, 1947

A homemade knee-block and leg brace,
and the mountains,
had given to Pete
what he'd come west to find.

He would never lose his gratitude
that he could ski
on his scarred legs
and with a numb left hand.

Each time
Pete Seibert laced up his boots
or looked at the sky,
so close he could almost touch it . . .

each time
he swept down a slope,
one with the mountain . . .

Pete was skiing for all of them:
the young men he'd trained with
at Camp Hale
but who'd not come home from the war.

Skiing!

There was nothing else like it in the world.

Pete Seibert skiing in Aspen, 1946. Due to his war injuries, his right turns were better than his left turns.

I wanted to ski at seventy
miles per hour and make
perfect turns . . . I thought
I could make it happen.

—PETE SEIBERT

That March,
Pete Seibert entered the biggest race of all:
the 1947 Roch Cup . . .

flying down the Roch Run
with the padded knee-block
and brace
wrapped beneath his pantleg.

Pete's amazing time:
twelve seconds ahead
of the next fastest skier.

The tiger on the hill
was back.

Pete with Gale "Spider" Spence (later a
noted racing coach) and Steve Knowlton
(far right) at the 1947 Roch Cup race. They
belonged to the Aspen Ski Club, a winter
sports club started in 1937, which became
the Aspen Valley Ski and Snowboard Club.
Today the club offers youth—from first-time
to top racers—lessons and training.

Breakfast in Aspen: Pete and Morrie Shepard with their mothers (Edythe Seibert on left and Helen Shepard on right) around 1948

With his fast race times,
Pete qualified for the
1950 U.S. Ski Team.

But when an ankle injury
sidelined him,
he looked past his life in Aspen
to the future.

The mountains had healed him,
and someday
he would find a mountain of his own.

As a soldier,
Pete knew training mattered.

So he boarded a ship for Europe,
to study at the famous École Hôtelière
in Lausanne, Switzerland.

At *his* ski resort,
he would need hotel skills
to be a fine innkeeper and host.

Pete (first row on far left) with the 1950 U.S. Men's Ski Team

Pete Seibert toured mountain towns
like Chamonix,
nestled in the French Alps,
to enter a few races
and ski the powder.

These were the places
he'd only imagined as a boy.

When Pete sailed back to America
with his hotel-school diploma,
he was ready to follow his dream.

To look ahead.

And make history happen.

CHAMONIX (Hte Savoie)
Téléférique du Brévent - Les Grands Charmoz
Le Grépon - Blaitière et l'Aiguille du Plan

PAR AVION

Seems as Though I come to Grenoble to pick up clean shirts and mail. Rec. The check and will send Tiny's. Am leaving this morning for a week in Spain at Barcelona and Nuria (The ski resort in the Pyrenees) Wonderful week at Chamonix! Sunshine every day. I took one of my most spectacular falls to date and therefore did not place to well in the Downhill. — will write from Spain Pete

MRS H. D. Steib
Box 652
ASPEN, Colo.
USA

In 1952, Pete sent this postcard to his
mother from Chamonix, France, in the Alps,
where he competed in downhill races. He
also went to Spain to ski in the Pyrenees.

The stars were still bright in the sky
when the two friends headed out
to scout a Colorado mountain.

It was March 19, 1957,
and Pete Seibert was thirty-two years old.

Earl Eaton,
a hunter and prospector
who loved sky and mountains
as much as Pete did,
was thirty-five.

For the past few years,
they'd hiked up a dozen other peaks
together . . .

looking for just the right one.

Earl had climbed this nameless mountain
the summer before
and told Pete that it held promise.

In the dark morning,
they strapped sealskins on their skis
to make the trek easier.

Earl Eaton, shown here in 1959, was a skier and adventurer who grew up in Colorado. He served in the U.S. Army in World War II.

Up and up Pete and Earl climbed,
knee-deep in powder
where no one had ever skied before,
and took turns breaking a trail.

The mountain was not far
from Camp Hale
and close to the Continental Divide.

Seven hours later,
when they reached the summit,
Pete leaned on his poles
and took in the spectacular view.
It was a moment he would always remember.

Everywhere he looked,
across the sloping terrain
and wide bowls filled with untracked snow,
Pete Seibert saw the outline
of his childhood dream.

There wasn't a town at the base.
Only sheep meadows.
But Pete would draw a design for one,
a town for skiers, with elegance and charm,
like those he'd seen in the Alps.

We've climbed all the way to heaven.

—PETE SEIBERT TO EARL EATON

Pete could picture it all.
He'd carried this vision
from Dr. Griffin's hill in Sharon
to war in the Apennines . . .

and back to the Rockies.

This was the mountain
on which to build his dream.

I'm proudest of the fact that I have a passion for life, and my passion happens to be for the mountains.

—PETE SEIBERT

Morrie Shepard trained as a U.S. Navy pilot in World War II and taught skiing in Aspen with Friedl Pfeifer after the war. Ski instruction was his calling. Here he carves a turn at Vail in the 1960s.

With one gondola
and two shiny chairlifts,
Vail Ski Resort
opened on December 15, 1962.

During that first season
Pete Seibert was everywhere.

As the manager,
he traversed the new slopes
and checked the depth of the snow
and greeted his guests
by name
with the welcome of a Swiss *hôtelier*.

Morrie Shepard was on the mountain
each day as well,
as director of the Vail Ski School.
Pete Seibert had chosen the best.

For a decade,
Pete had watched his oldest friend
instruct skiers of all ages
on the slopes of Aspen.
Morrie had a rare gift with his students
and carried teaching in his heart.

And Pete had kept the promise
he'd so often spoken to himself:
to create a ski resort for the future.
Now his hope was to share it with others.

On the bright slopes of Vail
and along its shadowed trails
where the snow
was crisp and deep,
Pete wanted every skier,
young and old,
to find and keep
the spirit of the sport he loved.

The wonder of it all . . .

of being *alive*
and part of something bigger . . .

the mountains.

**Pete Seibert moving
through powder, 1961**

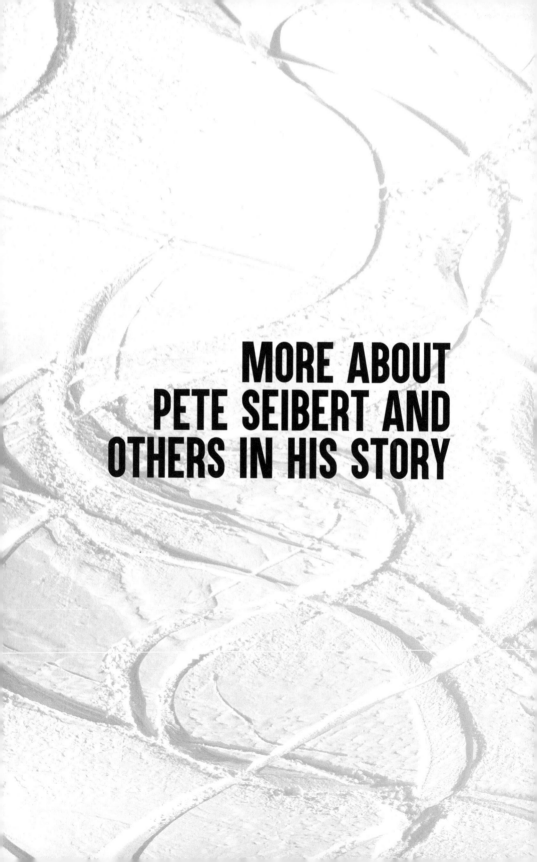

MORE ABOUT PETE SEIBERT AND OTHERS IN HIS STORY

Vail was named after a highway engineer who routed Highway 6 through its valley. It is now one of the most famous ski resorts in the world. Pete Seibert, who was awarded a Bronze Star and a Purple Heart in Italy, is known as the visionary who began Vail. Earl Eaton was the finder, and Pete was the founder.

In 1955, Pete married Betty Pardee and they began their family of three sons: Pete Jr., Brant, and Calvin. Pete was inducted into the Colorado Snowsports Museum Hall of Fame in 1980 and into the U.S. Ski and Snowboard Hall of Fame four years later.

Pete saw his children and grandchildren race at Vail and remained a skier until his death. He never lost his smile, and he had friends around the world.

Pete Seibert died from cancer on July 15, 2002, in Edwards, Colorado. Fifteen hundred people attended his funeral, including 10th Mountain veterans and a Vail pal of Pete's, the former President Gerald R. Ford.

Steve Knowlton skied in the 1948 Olympics at St. Moritz, Switzerland. He missed his chance to win a medal when he took a fall on the course. A member of the 1950 U.S. Ski team and of the U.S. Ski and Snowboard Hall of Fame, Steve died in 1998.

Howie Schless, the medic who rushed to Pete's side, was in the hospital in Martinsburg, West Virginia, in a body cast to heal his shoulder at the same time Pete Seibert was there. Howie, who had left Harvard to enlist in the 10th, recovered from his war wounds and returned to college, graduating with the class of 1949. He died in 1997.

Pete survived the battle on March 3, but Torger Tokle, the world's best ski jumper, so beloved by his 86th Regiment, did not. He died trying to knock out a German machine gun nest near Iola that day.

Percy Rideout, the Dartmouth College ski racer who served as Pete's company commander, was wounded in Italy and received a Purple Heart and a Bronze Star. He taught skiing in Aspen briefly after the war. Percy died in 2013 at age ninety-four.

Albert Seibert, Pete's father, died in 1947 of a heart attack, and Edythe Seibert, adored by Pete's ski friends, passed away in Denver in 1973. Christine, Pete's sister, an alumna of Smith College and later an artist of watercolors, married Green Penn and moved to North Carolina, where she died in June 2001.

After the war, Morrie Shepard went west to Aspen to join Pete. He served as the first director of the Vail Ski School. This was *his* joy, teaching skiers, as the famed Hannes Schneider had done decades before in North Conway, New Hampshire. A member of the Colorado Snowsports Museum Hall of Fame, Morrie lived with his wife, Suzie, in Eagle, Colorado, and Arizona. While skiing at Vail during Christmas of 2015, Morrie called the snow conditions *phenomenal*. He began 2017 by skiing on New Year's Day and passed away that year on October 12th.

Today in Sharon, Massachusetts, schoolchildren are still proud of Deborah Sampson when they walk down the street named in her honor. And they await the first snow so they can sled on Pettee's Hill, donated to the town by Dr. Walter Griffin.

The hill near Upland Road is no longer the same, and in Bartlett, New Hampshire, Stanton Slopes is a "lost ski area" in a neighborhood of homes. But many years ago, these places both shaped Pete Seibert's love of skiing.

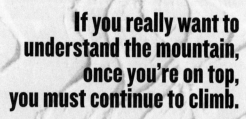

If you really want to understand the mountain, once you're on top, you must continue to climb.

—FRENCH MOUNTAIN GUIDE TO PETE SEIBERT

Skiers make their own paths
through the powder at Vail, 1981.

THE LEGACY OF
THE 10TH MOUNTAIN
DIVISION

The 10th Mountain Division first began in December, 1941, with the activation of the 87th Mountain Infantry Regiment at Fort Lewis, Washington, near Mount Rainier.

In 1942, the soldiers of the 87th moved to Colorado to train in the Rocky Mountains and by January of 1943, they had settled into a brand new army base, Camp Hale. With more recruits, the 85th and 86th regiments were soon formed. (The 87th left Camp Hale before Pete Seibert's arrival in Colorado and was later sent to the Aleutian Islands. There they liberated the island of Kiska from Japanese control in August, 1943. The 87th returned to Camp Hale in December, 1943 to continue training with the other two regiments.)

The 10th Mountain Division was made up of fourteen thousand men and included three infantry regiments (3,750 men each) plus field artillery groups, medical personnel, and one thousand engineers.

Each regiment had three battalions. Each battalion had five companies. Each company had four platoons, each with about forty to fifty soldiers. Platoons had four squads with ten to twelve soldiers.

Pete Seibert served in Company F, 2nd Battalion, 86th Mountain Infantry Regiment, 10th Mountain Division.

Two ski trails at Vail, Minnie's Mile (named after Minnie

Dole) and Riva Ridge, honor the soldiers of the 10th: those who died in combat* and those who came home.

A statue of a white-clad mountain trooper stands in the town of Vail.

At Aspen, skiers can ski the Roch Run or the black-diamond run named Seibert's.

Climbers and hikers can traverse miles of trails that link shelters in the 10th Mountain Division Hut System near the former site of Camp Hale. The base was officially closed in 1965.

Almost two thousand veterans of the 10th Mountain Division who came back from Italy chose to work as pioneers in the ski industry. Because of them, the sport of skiing expanded from New England to California. Sugarbush in Vermont, Lutsen Mountains in Minnesota, and sixty-two other resorts began with the hard work of 10th Mountain soldiers.

Some veterans became instructors, coaches, trail architects, and environmentalists. Some developed climbing equipment, clothes, and skis. One, Bill Bowerman, created a shoe with a waffle sole for the company he would cofound and that would later be called Nike.

They were ordinary Americans with vision. They were people who made history happen.

Years after the war, a group of 10th Mountain veterans returned to Vidiciatico for a reunion and climbed a trail in the Apennines with some German veterans to celebrate peace. Other 10th Mountain trips to Italy have continued into the twenty-first century.

George P. Hays retired from the U.S.

*During World War II, one thousand soldiers of the 10th Mountain Division lost their lives. Almost five thousand others were wounded.

Army with the rank of Lieutenant General. Highly respected by the soldiers who served under him, Hays died on August 7 (Pete Seibert's birthday), 1978, at the age of eighty-five. He is buried in Arlington National Cemetery in Washington, D.C.

Currently, soldiers of the 10th Mountain Division are based at Fort Drum, New York, and Fort Polk, Louisiana. Since the division's reactivation in 1985, soldiers of the 10th have served with distinction during Desert Shield/Storm, and in Somalia, Haiti, Bosnia, Kosovo, Afghanistan, Iraq, domestically, and in other smaller operations throughout the world. Today, the 10th remains on the front lines in the fight against members of the group known as ISIS, ISIL, or the Islamic State.

Corporal Michael Good, a 10th Mountain Division soldier, on patrol in the Nuristan province of Afghanistan, 2006

" ... the 10th Mountain gave American skiers a history. A past that they could look back at with pride, and a ... link from the past into the present and now into the future.

—BOB PARKER, VETERAN OF THE 10TH MOUNTAIN DIVISION AND A FRIEND OF PETE SEIBERT'S

CONNECTIONS

G rowing up, I spent every summer and also winter holidays in Leland, a harbor town in northern Michigan. There, one of my family's friends was a retired general, Mark W. Clark. I knew nothing about his famous role as commander of the American troops who liberated Rome during World War II—only that he loved to fish and whenever he stopped by our dock in his yellow boat my sisters and I addressed him as General.

Not far from Leland is Sugar Loaf Mountain—where I first learned to ski at age twelve. Decades later, while doing the research for *Ski Soldier*, I learned that a 10th Mountain Division veteran and Aspen ski instructor, Hans (Peppi) Teichner, was an early advisor to the founders of Sugar Loaf, where I mastered the snowplow and stem turn. Born in Germany, Peppi was a member of the German ski team and coached Spain's national ski team. After helping refugees escape to France

Louise Borden with Morrie Shepard in Colorado, 2017

over the Pyrenees during the Spanish Civil War, Peppi returned home to Nazi Germany but fled the country in 1937 because he was Jewish. He is often considered the father of skiing in lower Michigan.

Incredibly, I also found out that the headmaster of my school in Cincinnati, Francis W. Lovett, had served in the 10th Mountain Division as an 85th Regiment medic and received a Bronze Star in Italy, pinned on his uniform by General Mark Clark.

My connections to the 10th Mountain Division are part of the surprise, and wonder, of writing.

SOURCES

Asterisks (*) indicate sources for quotations that appear in *Ski Soldier*.

Books

Allen, E. John B. *From Skisport to Skiing: One Hundred Years of An American Sport, 1840–1940.* Amherst, MA: University of Massachusetts Press, 1993.

Atkeson, Ray, and Warren Miller. *Ski and Snow Country: The Golden Years of Skiing in the West, 1930s–1950s.* Portland, OR: Graphic Arts Center Publishing, 2000.

Behan, Tom. *The Italian Resistance.* London: Pluto Press, 2009.

Blumenson, Martin. *Mark Clark.* New York: Congdon & Weed, 1984.

Brooks, Thomas. *The War North of Rome, June 1944–May 1945.* New York: Sarpedon, 1996.

Burton, Hal. *The Ski Troops.* New York: Simon & Schuster, 1971.

Casewit, Curtis. *Mountain Troopers! The Story of the Tenth Mountain Division.* New York: Thomas Y. Crowell, 1972.

Dusenbery, Harris, and Wilson Ware. *Ski the High Trail: World War II Ski Troopers in the High Colorado Rockies.* Portland, OR: Binford & Mort Publishing, 1991.

Dusenbery, Harris. *The North Apennines and Beyond with the 10th Mountain Division.* Portland, OR: Binford & Mort Publishing, 1998.

Emtage, J. B. *Ski Fever.* London: Methuen, 1936.

Engen, Alan K. *For the Love of Skiing.* Salt Lake City: Gibbs Smith Publisher, 1998.

Facaros, Dana, and Michael Pauls. *Tuscany.* London: Cadogan Guides, 2002.

Fay, Abbott. *A History of Skiing in Colorado.* Ouray, CO: Western Reflections, 2000.

Feuer, A. B. *Packs On! Memoirs of the 10th Mountain Division in WW2.* Mechanicsburg, PA: Stackpole Books, 2004.

Gardini, T. L. *Towards the New Italy.* London: Lindsay Drummond, 1943.

171

Hampton, Chuck, ed. *An Illustrated Combat History of the U.S. 10th Mountain Division, 1944–1945*, 2001.

Holland, James. *Italy's Sorrow: A Year of War, 1944–1945*. New York: St. Martin's Press, 2008.

Huntford, Roland. *Two Planks and a Passion*. London and New York: Bloomsbury Academic, 2008.

Hauserman, Dick. *The Inventors of Vail*. Edwards, CO: Golden Peak Publishing, 2000.

Jenkins, McKay. *The Last Ridge*. New York: Random House, 2003.

Jones, Tom Lorang. *Colorado's Continental Divide Trail*. Englewood, CO: Westcliffe Publishers, 1997.

Koube, Caroline. *Florence and Tuscany*. London: New Holland Publishers, 2001.

Leich, Jeffrey R. *Tales of the 10th: The Mountain Troops and American Skiing*. Franconia, NH: New England Ski Museum, 2003.

Liz, Brian. *Colorado: Hut to Hut*. Englewood, CO: Westcliffe Publishers, 2000.

New Hampton School Yearbook, *The Belfry*, 1943.

Parker, Matthew. *Monte Cassino*. New York: Random House/ Anchor Books, 2004.

Parker, Robert W. *What'd You Do in the War, Dad?* Santa Fe: Rio Grande Publishing, 2005.

Sanders, Charles J. *The Boys of Winter*. Boulder, CO: University Press of Colorado, 2005.

*Seibert, Peter W., with William Oscar Johnson. *Vail: Triumph of a Dream*. Boulder, CO: Mountain Sports Press, 2000.

*Sharon High School Yearbook, *The Marsengold*, 1942.

Shelton, Peter. *Climb to Conquer: The Untold Story of the 10th Mountain Division Ski Troops*. New York: Scribner, 2003.

Turner Publishing Company. *10th Mountain Division*. Paducah, KY: Turner Publishing, 1998.

Wellborn, Charles. *History of the 86th Mountain Infantry in Italy*. Digitized and edited by Barbara Imbrie. 2004.

*Whitlock, Flint, and Bob Bishop. *Soldiers on Skis*. Boulder, CO: Paladin Press, 1992.

DVDs and videos

Fire on the Mountain: The Story of the 10th Mountain Division. First Run Features Home Video, New York (1995).

The Last Ridge: The Uphill Battles of the 10th Mountain Division. Janson Media, Irvington Park, New Jersey (2007).

Climb to Glory: WWII 10th Mountain Division in Italy (THA New Media, 2015). Warren Miller Entertainment, United States.

Oral-history interviews in the 10th Mountain Division Resource Center

*Typed transcripts and audio of Pete Seibert and Bob Parker interview by Martha Teichner (daughter of Hans "Peppi" Teichner) for *CBS Sunday Morning*, 1994 OH 244.

Audio of Steve Knowlton interview by Martha Teichner for *CBS Sunday Morning*, 1994 OH 217.

Audio and visual of Percy Rideout interview by Myrna Hampton, 2005 OH 369.

Typed transcript of Earl Clarke, Mac McKenzie, and Newcomb "Newc" Eldredge interview by Martha Teichner for *CBS Sunday Morning*, 1994 OH 313.

Newspaper and magazine articles

*Buck, Cindy. "Carving a Mountain." *The Hamptonia* (New Hampton School), Spring 1998.

*Meadows, James B. "The Visionary of Vail." *Rocky Mountain News*, March 30, 2002.

Thruelsen, Richard. "The 10th Caught It All at Once." *Saturday Evening Post*, December 8, 1945.

Ware, Wilson. "The Riva Ridge." *American Alpine Journal* 6, no. 2 (1946).

Issues of *The Blizzard*, newspaper of the 10th Mountain Division begun in 1944: no. 2 (Italy, February 27, 1945); no. 3 (Italy, March 7, 1945); no. 4 (Italy, March 15, 1945); no. 9 (Italy, June 10, 1945).

Author's conversations or correspondence with veterans and friends

Francis Lovett
Hugh Evans
*Morrie and Suzie Shepard
Nick Dann
Shirley Schofield
Pete Seibert Jr.
Debbie Gemar
Dennis Hagen
Keli Schmid
Laura Penn-Eckman
Doug Schmidt

A WONDERFUL TEAM

I would like to thank Debbie Gemar, Dennis Hagen, and the amazing Keli Schmid at the Denver Public Library; Jordan Halter and Vail Resorts; the Colorado Snowsports Museum (Vail); generous Jeff Leich and the New England Ski Museum (Franconia, NH); the Vermont Ski and Snowsports Museum (Stowe, VT); the Aspen Historical Society; Norman Head and the Bartlett Historical Society; and Shirley Schofield and the Sharon Historical Society.

Special thanks to Pete Seibert Jr., Laura Penn-Eckman (the daughter of Christine Louise Seibert Penn), Francis Lovett, Morrie and Suzie Shepard, Nick Dann, Hugh Evans, Wilson Ware and his wartime sketches, Harris Dusenbery for his inspiring accounts, Martha Teichner, Bob Parker, Sarah DeBenedictis and the New Hampton School, Barbara Waters and Karen Gustafson at Kennett Schools (North Conway, NH), Judy Williams (who took me to Camp Hale), Pete Borden (who drove me to the Florence American Cemetery and Memorial, and around mountain curves to Vidiciatico), Bruno Bartolome at the Monte Grande Hotel (Vidiciatico), and Marc and Cate Cohen (who skied Riva Ridge at Vail with me).

Blue sky days also to fellow skiers Cindy and Alex Curchin, Ted Borden, Abigail and Henry Cohen, Ashley Wolff, Jill Colaw, and future skiers Brooks and Caroline Ehret; Vermont pals Kathi and Bob Roesler and Sissy Stearns; the kind staff at Saxby's; encouragers Amy Flynn, Loren Long, Sydney McCurdy, Maryann Macdonald, Trish Marx, Beth Fotheringill, Cris Tovani, Steph Harvey, Ellen Ruffin, M. K. Kroeger, Barb Libby, Connie Trounstine, George Ella Lyon, Mary Sexton, Franki Sibberson, Ayars and Matt Ehret, Jane Paul, the Graces, Kathryn Lewis, Johanna Hurwitz, Terri Pytlik; my steady Dublin friends; and those Hardy sisters who cheer me on from Massachusetts and Mississippi.

A thousand salutes to my fearless editor, Carolyn Yoder, a native of New England who climbed Riva Ridge in countless drafts; to wise Lori A. Lyons and Katarina Rice; to Red Herring Design; to the team at Calkins Creek; and to my steadfast agent and Vail skier, Elizabeth Harding, for her belief in *Ski Soldier*.

PICTURE CREDITS

Aspen Historical Society: 138, 139, 140, 142–143, 145, 148–149

Bartlett Historical Society: 26–27

Denver Public Library, 10th Mountain Division: 1, 45, 46, 49, 50, 52, 53, 55, 56–57, 60, 62 (top), 64–65, 78–79, 81, 82–83, 89, 91, 93, 94, 96–97, 98–99, 113, 114–115, 123, 166

Laura Penn-Eckman: 14, 146–147

Louise Borden: 169

Morrie and Suzie Shepard: 34

National Archives and Records Administration: 86–87

New England Ski Museum: 24–25, 28, 30–31, 36

New Hampton School: 40–41, 42–43, 44

Shutterstock.com: 5, 6–7, 10–11, 12, 21, 66–67, 73, 76, 126–127, 130–131, 137, 160–161, 164–165

Seibert Family: 17, 47, 151, 153

United States Army: 62 (bottom), 167

Vail Resorts: 156, 159, 163